ALEXANDER WILLIAM SALTER

THE SPIRIT
—— OF ——

LIBERTARIANISM &
AMERICAN RENEWAL

AIER | AMERICAN INSTITUTE
for ECONOMIC RESEARCH

ALEXANDER
WILLIAM SALTER

THE SPIRIT
—— OF ——

LIBERTARIANISM &
AMERICAN RENEWAL

AMERICAN INSTITUTE FOR ECONOMIC RESEARCH

The Spirit of '76: Libertarianism and American Renewal
By Alexander William Salter

Copyright © 2023 by The American Institute for Economic Research,
Creative Commons Attribution International 4.0.

ISBN: 9781630692285

Design: Vanessa Mendozzi

CONTENTS

INTRODUCTION

"A nation which makes greatness its polestar can never be free," warned Abraham Bishop, a friend and supporter of Thomas Jefferson. "Beneath national greatness sink individual greatness, honor, wealth, and freedom."[1] These words could have been written today. Bombasity masquerading as grandiosity has consumed American politics. The right venerates the power of the nation-state; the left sings the praises of fashionable corporations and NGOs; both trample the human person in their frenzy for greatness.

I wrote this book to defend the old American ideals of "honor, wealth, and freedom." Honor—not pride, but a life of integrity; wealth—not indulgence, but the right use of creation's bounty; freedom—not licentiousness, but ordered liberty in the soul and commonwealth. Americans appreciate the creative tension between rights and responsibilities. Until recently, we knew liberty without order was decadent and order without liberty was tyrannical. But many powerful and influential figures have decided this wisdom is obsolete because it obstructs their demands for "systemic equity" or their desire to "own the libs."

They're wrong. Ordered liberty defines America. We cannot become great *as Americans* by ignoring who we are.

The essays in this book first appeared as a series of opinion articles in the *Lubbock Avalanche-Journal*. The theme of the series is libertarianism: An unapologetic defense of liberty as America's greatest *political* good. I wanted to explain the philosophy of liberty in terms everybody could understand. Public affairs shouldn't

---

1 Abraham Bishop. 1800. *An oration on the extent and power of political delusion.* Newark, NJ: Pennington and Gould.

be the exclusive domain of political operatives and intellectuals. Self-governance is essential for liberty; public deliberation about important issues and ideas must be the domain of the many, not the few. There are some things we must never "outsource" to experts, at risk of relinquishing our humanity. Governing the nation is one of them.

I had three goals in writing these essays. The book's structure reflects those goals. Part I covers the history of American liberty. By surveying how it was pursued, debated, and enshrined, I wanted to remind my countrymen of liberty's central place in American public affairs. That also means coming to terms with major turns away from liberty. The Progressive revolution of the early 20th century is an obvious case. But the struggle for liberty is much older than that. Even the ratification of the U.S. Constitution was a mixed blessing for freedom. It did not spring fully-formed from the heads of the Founding Fathers. Rather it was the culmination of an unsteady process, with power politics and fiscal-military ambitions mixed in. Nevertheless, the Constitution deserves our respect and loyalty. To revive American liberty, we must renew rather than repudiate its spirit.

Part II explores the philosophy of liberty. Libertarianism affirms a natural-rights approach to politics. Each person has the right to be free from force and fraud. Too often, we defend these rights in private but overlook them in public. But if anything, it's more important to prevent rights-violations by the government, for the simple reason that the government is much stronger than any private entity. (To those fretting over Big Tech: Please remember Twitter can delete your account without consequence, but Uncle Sam can kill you without consequence.) Recognizing the disproportionate threat the government poses to liberty, we can better appreciate the difference between law and morality, the religious roots of human dignity, and the complementarity of freedom and order.

I turn from philosophy to policy in Part III. We desperately need a libertarian perspective on national problems such as unsustainable government spending and entitlements, misguided health care programs, a broken immigration system, and reckless foreign policy. At home and abroad, the government has become dysfunctional because we've forgotten its proper scale and scope. It's become trendy in some circles to dismiss liberty-focused reforms as "zombie Reaganism" or "market fundamentalism." These are unserious criticisms. Certainly, libertarianism appreciates the contributions of free enterprise to human flourishing. But civil society, the crucial domain between markets and states, matters just as much. So does federalism: Local governments will be important players in securing responsible and freedom-respecting reforms. Far from reifying "atomistic individualism," libertarian policy is both realistic and communal. It's time we relearned how to govern ourselves, rather than passing the buck to Washington, DC.

A constitutional republic dedicated to ordered liberty is a great blessing. We do not consent to be ruled by insular oligarchs, pretentious mandarins, or an unruly mob. We do not consent to be *ruled* at all. Instead, we agree to be *governed*—public reason under the rule of law has the final say. Defenders of freedom and virtue have recently taken a beating in politics, but libertarianism can get us back in the fight. I hope these essays leave you with an appreciation for what makes the American experiment unique and worthy of continued loyalty.

Alexander William Salter
Lubbock, TX | January 2023

PART I

THE HISTORY OF AMERICAN LIBERTY

CONSERVING LIBERTY:
Why Libertarianism Deserves a Hearing

"I believe the very heart and soul of conservatism is libertarianism."[2] This sentiment was expressed by President Ronald Reagan, whose conservative bona fides need no defense. My readers are likely with conservatism. But what is this strange idea, libertarianism? Answering this question illuminates much of what's wrong with contemporary politics.

Conservatism is a philosophy of life with political implications. Russell Kirk, the godfather of American conservatism in the years following World War II, argued conservatism was defined by a commitment to moral realism and a belief in a transcendent sanction for the social order. In contrast, the scope of libertarianism is more limited. Libertarianism is a political philosophy: Its domain is the relationship between man and the state. Libertarians affirm *liberty* as the highest goal of politics. In other words, the purpose of the state is to make men free and preserve them in freedom.

Libertarians are often dismissed as libertines. Supposedly they only desire freedom so they can remain unmolested in their hedonistic pursuits. If you've ever heard the joke, "A libertarian is a conservative who likes marijuana," you're familiar with this critique. But this is a straw man. Certainly, some libertarians desire

---

2 Manuel Klausner. 1975. "Inside Ronald Reagan." *Reason*, July.

liberty for unsavory purposes. But you can find people of low character in *any* political movement. For most libertarians, the thirst for liberty is part of a deep commitment to protecting man's God-given rights and promoting human flourishing.

Why did President Reagan say libertarianism was the heart of conservatism? This hearkens back to an old debate in American political thought. Is the purpose of politics virtue or liberty? In other words, is it the job of the state to make us good, or to make us free? On the one hand, freedom must be used to pursue virtue if we are to reach our full potential. On the other hand, virtue must be freely chosen, or else it is not to our credit. Reagan's sentiment expressed a noble attempt to reconcile these tensions. The philosophy known as *fusionism* held that liberty and virtue could each find their proper place.

Liberty is the end of government, but virtue is the end of civil society. Man's ultimate goal is to become virtuous. The state helps us do this by carving out a space in which families, churches, fraternal organizations, and many other associations can freely help us reach our moral potential. According to fusionism, liberty and virtue are complements, not substitutes.

Fusionism was, once upon a time, the dominant position on the American right. But it always held more sway among intellectuals and philosophers than public servants. Although American politicians and bureaucrats paid homage to the tenets of fusionism, they rarely practiced what they preached. The proof is that even when self-proclaimed conservatives held political power, government kept getting bigger and bigger, trampling liberty underfoot.

Today, American conservatives are much less enthusiastic about liberty. A nationalist and populist fervor has swept conservative politics. The motivation behind this new movement is certainly understandable: A belief that insular and self-serving elites have captured American public institutions, robbing citizens of their rightful voice in public affairs. Although they recognize the problem, their solutions are a mirage. Nowadays conservatives are eager to demand "an eye for an eye and a tooth for a tooth," but we cannot renew America through violence and strife.

This is why libertarianism matters. We need to make a full-throated defense of liberty, of the principles of the American Revolution. Our Declaration of Independence, perhaps the most libertarian political document ever written, proclaims the "self-evident" truths that "all men are created equal" and that "they are endowed by their Creator with certain unalienable rights, that among these are Life, Liberty, and the pursuit of Happiness." This should appeal to conservatives, too. After all, what could be more important to conserve than our Founding principles?

President Reagan was fond of John Winthrop's evocative metaphor of America as a "city upon a hill."[3] America has always been a beacon of liberty to the world. Libertarianism means a whole-hearted commitment to continuing our noble experiment with lawful self-government. At a time when our nation faces unprecedented challenges, many right-wingers are calling for an active and vigorous federal government to solve our nation's problems in top-down fashion. They forget that liberty is our birthright. By abandoning it, we become less than ourselves.

The Preamble to our Constitution asserts its purpose is to "secure the blessings of liberty to ourselves and our posterity." Libertarianism, as a philosophy, is wholeheartedly devoted to this endeavor. Now more than ever, the philosophy of freedom deserves a hearing.

---

3 John Winthrop. 1630. "A Model of Christian Charity." March 21.

THE SPIRIT OF '76:
Libertarianism and the Declaration of Independence

Libertarianism is a rational reconstruction of America's founding principles. It's as American as apple pie. You don't need to take my word for it. The Declaration of Independence proclaims the importance of liberty in nearly every sentence.

Remember, the United States was born in an uprising against tyranny. This truth reveals why libertarianism matters for contemporary American politics. Regardless of the questionable prudence of securing liberty through rebellion—a strategy that has a rather unimpressive track record—the American colonists-turned-citizens won their freedom, including the right to govern themselves. Both freedom from *any* government, as well as the right to choose *our* government, are important components of liberty, and hence libertarianism.

We all know the Declaration's most famous passage: "We hold these truths to be self-evident, that all men are created equal, that they are endowed by their Creator with certain unalienable Rights, that among these are Life, Liberty and the pursuit of Happiness." This is a beautiful and concise statement of libertarian philosophy. All human beings have rights upon which nobody may trespass. Neither private individuals nor public agents can take what others are due, as a matter of justice. Furthermore, our rights are not handed down to us by the government. We possess them in virtue of our humanity and the inherent dignity that comes with it.

Moreover, "to secure these rights, Governments are instituted among Men, deriving their just powers from the consent of the governed." We take this idea for granted today. But it was quite radical in 1776! In declaring to the world their reasons for seeking independence, Thomas Jefferson and the other Founding Fathers asserted the state exists to serve man, not man to serve the state. The Founders believed in virtue and piety. They would never reject their civic duty or moral obligation to serve their fellow men. Instead, they asserted a limited scope for government in securing human flourishing. As Jefferson wrote elsewhere, defenders of liberty deny anybody is "born with saddles on their backs, nor a favored few booted and spurred, ready to ride them legitimately, by the grace of God."[4]

Governments everywhere too easily become oppressive. Power tends towards concentration, and the state is the ultimate form of coercive power. When the government oversteps its bounds, "it is the Right of the People to alter or to abolish it, and to institute new Government, laying its foundation on such principles and organizing its powers in such form, as to them shall seem most likely to effect their Safety and Happiness." Obviously, this is an extreme remedy. Losing an election, or even several elections, isn't a good enough reason to grab your musket. Nevertheless, a core tenet of libertarianism is citizens' right to discipline the state when it tramples human dignity.

These three principles animate libertarianism. Libertarians passionately believe in man's natural rights, foremost among them the right to be free from force and fraud. Libertarians assert an instrumental function for government: It should be judged according to its defense of natural rights. And libertarians hold government officials are agents of the citizenry, nothing more. Hence if politicians and bureaucrats get too big for their britches, it's good and proper to

---

4 Thomas Jefferson. 1826. "Letter to Roger C. Weightman." June 24.

send them packing. Libertarianism is a consistent witness to, and defense of, the Principles of '76.

Libertarians' ideological foes often claim they believe in these principles. Conservatives (the right) and progressives (the left) each see themselves as the inheritors of the American tradition. But in crucial ways, both violate natural rights by using government coercion to advance their own goals. Conservatives are far too quick to overlook rights violations committed by domestic law enforcement and the military. Progressives ignore the ways their reckless taxing, spending, and regulatory plans violate property rights. Even more concerningly, both deny the right to speak and gather freely when they disagree with the speakers' and gatherers' purposes.

For libertarians, all rights violations are unacceptable. If we only defend peoples' rights when we approve of their behavior, then we don't really believe in universal human dignity. Rather we believe in a transitory and conditional dignity, which exists only if other people like what we like and do what we do. Nothing could be more inimical to freedom. The Founders rightly rejected this servile philosophy. Libertarians honor them by continuing their work.

"Freedom is never more than one generation away from extinction," warned President Reagan.[5] Citizens must never rest on their laurels. Freedom wasn't achieved once and for all in 1776. Liberty must be "fought for, protected, and passed on" to our posterity. Thankfully, we don't need an armed uprising or a divisive, us-versus-them mentality to keep our freedoms. For all its faults, the American political system is responsive to the demands of its citizens. Liberty is a fire that has lit the minds and hearts of men for hundreds of years. Libertarians are proud to tend that flame, in the hope that equal liberty for all may one day be ours.

---

5 Ronald Reagan. 1964. "The Speech." October 27.

LIBERTY FORGOTTEN:
The Articles of Confederation

America's political tradition is founded on liberty. But our freedom means much more than "rugged individualism" or "cowboy capitalism." American liberty is *ordered* liberty. Americans demand freedom so they can be the best version of themselves. Libertarianism carries forward this honorable tradition into the 21st century.

Liberty flourishes where government is strictly limited in scale and scope. The essence of government is violence. Sometimes that violence is used for good purposes, as when a police officer stops a robbery. But it is violence, nonetheless. Because government power is often abused, it's a very good idea to keep the state on a tight leash. "Government is not reason, it is not eloquence—it is force!" George Washington reputedly said. "Like fire it is a dangerous servant and a fearful master." President Washington understood well the nature of government.

We need conscious constitutional craftsmanship to preserve freedom. Alexander Hamilton said it best: It is up to Americans to show the world whether mankind can establish "good government from reflection and choice, or whether they are forever destined to depend for their political constitutions on accident and force."[6] Tradition is good. Folkways are good. But by themselves, they

---

6 Alexander Hamilton. 1787. "General Introduction." *The Independent Journal*, October 27.

cannot guarantee liberty. We have both the right and duty to take the reins of government in hand to secure the blessings of liberty.

The U.S. Constitution is rightly venerated for creating a government of ordered liberty. But the Constitution wasn't our first constitution. We need to do a little historical digging to recover the nation's earliest governing charter: The Articles of Confederation. Without appreciating the virtues of this document, we won't fully understand our own story.

The American colonies-turned-states ratified the Articles of Confederation on March 15, 1781. The Articles governed the nation from its most tumultuous days in its conflict with Great Britain until the Constitution was ratified in 1789. Unlike the Constitution's federal government, the *confederal* government under the Articles was strictly limited. 9 out of 13 states had to agree for an act of the unicameral Congress to pass. Amending the articles required unanimity. Most important was Article II, which explicitly laid out the nature of the government as a voluntary association of states: "Each state retains its sovereignty, freedom, and independence, and every power, jurisdiction, and right, which is not by this Confederation expressly delegated to the United States, in Congress assembled."

From a libertarian standpoint, the Articles of Confederation was an impressive document. The confederation had no power to impose taxes, maintain a standing army or navy, or regulate commerce. Today's Americans have learned the hard way that taxes can become punitive, armies and navies can be instruments of imperialism, and commercial regulations are often the excuse used by Washington to micromanage our lives. Perhaps our Founding Fathers had it right the first time around! As E. James Ferguson, a respected historian of the early Republic wrote, our first constitution emphasized "defense of local rights against central authority. The Articles were designed to safeguard liberty."[7]

---

7 E. James Ferguson. 1968. *The Power of the Purse: A History of American Public Finance, 1776-1790*. Williamsburg, VA: Omohundro Institutte and University of North Carolina Press, p. 111.

But wasn't American government dysfunctional under the Articles? Critics contended the new nation couldn't pay its war debt, excessive decentralization resulted in the states engaging in costly trade wars with each other, and the high concurrence requirements for Congressional action hampered valuable political projects. But all these claims are exaggerated. The states themselves, not the confederation government, took the lead on paying the war debt. Trade barriers between states were minimal. And the whole point of the Articles was to discourage political projects unless they were truly in the interest of the whole nation.

The constitutional theory of the Articles was simple: Keep government constrained! Most politics should happen at the state and local level. National politics is only for those rare occasions where the entire nation must act collectively. Even then, there needs to be explicit consent with greater-than-majority voting thresholds. Anything else threatens the liberty Americans just shed blood to win. The only real strike against the Articles is that the confederation could not withstand the political ambitions of those among the Federalist faction who hungered for national greatness, possible only with a stronger and more activist central government.

"Somewhere in the course of American democracy the nation at large forgot to distinguish between the government and the people," Ferguson lamented. "Individual rights and local privileges were no longer regarded as standing against the authority of the government; they were to be advanced by soliciting its aid and patronage."[8] We lost something priceless when we abandoned the Articles for the Constitution. That doesn't mean we forfeited the promise of liberty in America. But it does mean we must turn a critical eye to our own history, to ensure our hard-won rights are not taken away.

---

8 Ibid., p. 234.

4

THE CONSTITUTION AND LIBERTY

In a democracy, public policy rests on the consent of the governed. The great economist James Buchanan, who won the Nobel Prize in 1986, wrote that democratic consensus matters because it's the point of departure from which debates about policy changes proceed. Our starting point, here and now, is the U.S. Constitution: Its text, duly ratified amendments, and judicially interpreted meaning.

For lovers of liberty, the Constitution is an impressive document. Although lacking in some ways compared to the Articles of Confederation, our current national charter has the clear benefit of durability. The Constitution has been the basic law of the land for 232 years. Many of those years were prosperous. Some were tumultuous and destructive. The Constitution endured it all. It provides the bulwark of order against which liberty stands.

Libertarians like me admire the Constitution. We just wish our fellow citizens admired it as much as we do! While the Constitution isn't a fully libertarian document, it's arguably the most pro-freedom compact in existence. When libertarians have a problem with the Constitution, it's usually because too many politicians, bureaucrats, and even voters ignore parts of the text they don't like.

The ways in which the Constitution protects freedom are obvious. Separation of powers and checks and balances are built into the system. This makes it very difficult for political coalitions to seize absolute control of the government. And even if they do, the Bill of

Rights, buttressed by the courts, stands guard over the citizenry. We Americans cherish our rights to speak freely, assemble freely, worship freely. We take pride in our protections against arbitrary seizure of property. And we know that these rights are *natural* rights, given to us by God. The Constitution recognizes them, but does not establish them.

In fact, the 9th Amendment explicitly says this: "The enumeration in the Constitution, of certain rights, shall not be construed to deny or disparage others retained by the people." In other words, the rights of the people are far too numerous to list. Just because the Framers didn't write down a specific right doesn't mean we don't have that right. The Constitution is meant to limit the government, not the citizens.

The 10th Amendment also supports liberty: "The powers not delegated to the United States by the Constitution, nor prohibited by it to the States, are reserved to the States respectively, or to the people." While libertarians lament the omission of the word "expressly" from this amendment, it's nonetheless a demonstration of the Founders' fondness for federalism. That government which governs best governs closest to the citizens.

What parts of the Constitution do libertarians dislike? There are a few: The Necessary and Proper Clause, the Commerce Clause, and an unlimited power of taxation are the most obvious examples. The Necessary and Proper Clause, unless carefully interpreted, could easily result in an almost-unlimited federal government. Likewise, the Commerce Clause has been used to justify federal meddling in any situation which could conceivably—even hypothetically!—affect trade across the United States. The lack of strict controls on the taxing power has resulted in tax rates that are downright confiscatory. All of these yield a government that is too big, too intrusive, and too powerful.

But we oughtn't throw the baby out with the bathwater. The Constitution remains a respectable governance framework for a free and virtuous people. We can work within the Constitutional system to preserve its strengths and shore up its weaknesses.

Unfortunately, the greatest obstacle to Constitutional renewal is the mass of politicians who are sworn to uphold it.

Republicans and Democrats are quick to praise the Constitution on the campaign trail or at a fundraiser. But when it comes to governing, their policies are a Constitutional disgrace. One is reminded of the prophecy of Isaiah: "These people come near to me with their mouth and honor me with their lips, but their hearts are far from me." The sad reality is that government-run-amok is a bipartisan consensus. No party believes in keeping Washington, DC within the bounds of the Constitution. Many libertarians became libertarian because they've had enough of our political duopoly's two-step between pro-Constitutional rhetoric and anti-Constitutional policy.

The Constitution isn't perfect. No governing document is. But thanks to the Constitution, life, liberty, and property have been reasonably secure in the United States for more than two centuries. Libertarians seek to rein in the federal government by forcing it to follow the law of the land. While we can be reformist in our political programs, we must be radical in our aims.

American exceptionalism comes down to the rule of law: The idea that governed and governors alike must play by the same rules. Libertarians demand, as a matter of natural right, nothing less than the restoration of the rule of law. A crucial first step is to reinstate Constitutional constraints on government.

LIBERTY ABANDONED:
We're All Progressives Now

American liberty is in trouble. Our national debt as a percentage of GDP has reached levels not seen since World War II. A vast regulatory bureaucracy implements mountains of new rules restricting Americans' freedom. Congress is consumed by partisan showboating. The national government crowds out state and local governments, reducing effectiveness and accountability. The Founders didn't risk their "lives, fortunes, and sacred honor" for this!

What went wrong? As uncomfortable as it is to admit, liberty doesn't rank very high on Americans' priority list. Even deep red districts, where electing a Democrat is unthinkable, regularly send Republicans to Washington who have no problem expanding government control over our lives. Ordered liberty has few passionate and principled defenders.

As a libertarian, I find this frustrating. When it comes to freedom, why do so many of my countrymen talk the talk but refuse to walk the walk? I doubt there's a single answer. Public opinion is a slippery, complex thing. But we know ideas matter. If we can identify how ideas changed, we can start to understand how public opinion changed.

In terms of ideas, one transformation looms large in American history: The rise of Progressivism and its domination of the U.S. political landscape.

Progressivism is devoted to government-led social improvement. It is simultaneously optimistic and pessimistic. Its optimistic tenet is that society is perpetually improvable. Its pessimistic tenet is that the public can't be trusted to improve itself. Thus Progressivism endorses a centrally and hierarchically administered state, controlled by an enlightened governing class. Whereas the traditional American conception of statecraft relied on democratic self-governance, Progressive governance is necessarily the prerogative of an elite few.

The Progressive revolution swept through American institutions during late 19th and early 20th centuries. The earliest Progressive reforms started at the state level, but it didn't take long for ambitious politicians and social crusaders to set their sights on Washington. The administrations of Presidents Wilson and Roosevelt (Franklin, though Theodore was a Progressive, too) spearheaded a Constitutional revolution: The Executive branch grew more powerful at the expense of the Legislative branch, and the national government grew more powerful at the expense of state and local governments.

Today's government reflects the institutional legacy of Progressivism. We assume the national government matters more than state and local governments and the president matters more than Congress. Federalism and representative government are out; nationalism and administrative government are in. Progressivism also colors our ideological battles. Left-wing politicians openly identify as Progressives. Right-wing politicians style themselves conservatives, but all they're trying to "conserve" is Progressivism. There's actually little ideological disagreement in this country. We're not arguing over a fundamental difference in political philosophy. We're just haggling over who gets to be in charge for a little while.

Many Americans, especially Republicans, say they dislike Progressivism. But their actions belie their words. Do we really understand the changes necessary to roll back the Progressive revolution? Let's just consider the size of government for a moment. Early in the 20th century, before Progressivism won, government as a fraction of the economy was a mere 10%. Furthermore, only a third of that was the national government. The rest was state and local governments. Today, however, government is approximately 30% of the economy. Washington is now about two thirds of that. Talk about topsy-turvy!

It's easy to mouth pro-liberty platitudes. We carry copies of the Constitution in our pockets and wave flags on the Fourth of July. Come election season, we tell ourselves *this time* we'll "drain the swamp" and get Washington under control. But when we cast our ballots, the truth comes out: Scratch a "patriot" and what shows underneath is just a right-wing Progressive.

Not even President Reagan was ambitious enough to reverse the legacies of Wilson and Roosevelt. Perhaps he should've been. His conservative-libertarian coalition had a shot, and even made some pro-freedom reforms, but in the end proved unwilling or unable to change the government's basic structure. That's a shame. Most of our political problems stem from a bloated government. Uncle Sam has become a red giant: It's tepid and ineffective *because* it's too big. If we want a lean, mean government that's able to tackle the challenges of the 21st century, the place to start is to cut it down to size.

The pretend contests between left-Progressive Democrats and right-Progressive Republicans won't solve our problems. Both parties accept a flawed premise: The public can be better served by the Progressive vision than the Founding vision. Are we willing to do the hard work to govern ourselves, or are we okay taking our marching orders from Washington? The latter is a fundamentally servile attitude. The former represents what's best in America's tradition of ordered liberty.

REDISCOVERING FREEDOM

The task of 21st century statesmanship is restoring limited, lawful government. Government has run amok since the Progressive Era. This is easiest to see at the national level, but often state and local governments could use a rollback, too. Politics can't solve all our problems, or even most of our problems. A self-governing society doesn't delegate the responsibilities of living to politicians and bureaucrats. Uncle Sam gorged himself on our watch. Now it's up to We the People to put him on a diet.

Shrinking government's scale and scope is clearly a libertarian goal. For libertarians, the proper end of government is liberty, which means freedom from force and fraud. There's great wisdom in this conception of liberty. Public aggression is just as deplorable as private aggression. By applying the same rules to governors and governed, we reject a moral double standard. Thus in public life, as in private life, we stand on civilized terms with our neighbors when we seek their consent. We should try to persuade our fellow citizens when we disagree, not coerce them. And if we can't persuade them, we should think very carefully before using politics to force a resolution.

What if you're not a libertarian? Even then, you have an interest in shrinking the state. It's no secret our politics is highly polarized. We don't just disagree about policy. We're coming dangerously close to believing political disagreement is a *moral failure*. In some ways we're already there. The nation can't hold together if each half of the political spectrum views the other as illegitimate. "A house divided against itself cannot stand."[9] The stakes of politics are just too high.

So, let's lower the stakes! If government is constrained by respect for liberty and the plain meaning of the Constitution, we can all get along. Losing an election isn't a big deal if the winners can't do the losers much harm. If government operated on libertarian principles, it'd be safer for everyone to let bygones be bygones. Losing factions can pick themselves up, dust themselves off, and get ready for the next election, comforted by the fact that their opponents' worst actions are off the table.

Politics is rough. We'll never play the game according to Marquess of Queensberry rules. But it doesn't have to be total war. Libertarianism is the answer to our ongoing political arms race.

You may be familiar with the 1983 film *WarGames*. In the movie, the protagonist (played by Matthew Broderick) hacks into a military computer without realizing it. Everything seems like fun and games until the computer brings the U.S. and the Soviet Union to the brink of nuclear war. Some quick thinking by the young hacker persuades the computer that nuclear war has no winners. "A strange game," the computer muses. "The only winning move is not to play."

Just so. All-or-nothing politics is another kind of arms race. If the stakes of politics are low—if everything that's up for grabs is, say, how much funding an interstate highway extension gets—there's no reason to demonize our opponents. But if the stakes are nothing less than a comprehensive moral vision for the nation, backed by the guns of the state, each side is one lost election away from going to the mattresses. Remember the charged rhetoric about the "Flight 93 election" on the right, or "democracy on the ballot" on the left? That's exactly what we want to avoid.

We can't live in peace like this. Instead, we need politics to promote social harmony. When we cooperate with our neighbors,

---

9 Abraham Lincoln. 1858. *Speech of Hon. Abram Lincoln before the Republican state convention, June 16, 1858.* Sycamore, IL: O.P. Bassett.

we can do great things, both privately and publicly. This makes libertarianism uniquely attractive as a political philosophy. Even if you're not sold on the moral worth of individual liberty, I'm confident you see the value of unity among countrymen! Totalizing politics, whether right-wing or left-wing, turns friends into enemies. Liberty turns enemies into friends. It's better to have friends.

Americans must rediscover the value of freedom. There's so much good that can be done if we embrace liberty. Our nation's past shows the glory that freedom makes possible, as well as the misery that follows when freedom fades. National discord and stagnation aren't our destiny. President Reagan was right when he warned that liberty is never more than a generation away from extinction. But this also means it's never more than a generation away from rebirth.

Conservatives want to Make America Great Again, but forget that liberty made America great in the first place. Progressives want to Build Back Better, but by rejecting liberty, they foolishly build atop sand. For Americans, freedom is what we should conserve and what we should progress towards. Libertarianism offers us civic peace through humane politics. If we choose freedom, it's the next century, not the last one, that we'll remember as the American Century.

PART II

THE PHILOSOPHY OF LIBERTY

LIBERTY AND THE ESSENCE
OF GOVERNMENT

Why are libertarians so wary of government? Isn't government just another name for the things we do together?

No, actually, it isn't.

We need to take a closer look at the essence of the state. The philosophy of liberty–meaning the philosophy of the American Founding, refined to meet contemporary challenges–helps us understand why, for our own safety's sake, we need to keep government strictly limited.

"Society in every state is a blessing," wrote Thomas Paine. "But government even in its best state is but a necessary evil."[10] If there's a one-sentence summary of the philosophy of liberty, this is it. Libertarians are constantly on guard against confounding society and the state. Unlike society, the state is fundamentally coercive.

Force and fraud are the two biggest threats to civic harmony. It's appropriate for government to crack down on these antisocial acts. Government's enforcement power comes from its ability to cause lawbreakers physical harm. But we can't ignore the possibility that government itself may become a lawbreaker. As James Madison

10 Thomas Paine. 1776. *Common Sense: Addressed to the Inhabitants of America, on the following Interesting Subjects, viz.: I. Of the Origin and Design of Government in General; with Concise Remarks on the English Constitution. II. Of Monarchy and Hereditary Succession. III. Thoughts on the Present State of American Affairs. IV. Of the Present Ability of America; with some Miscellaneous Reflections.* Philadelphia: R. Bell.

wisely said, we must "enable the government to control the governed" and "oblige it to control itself" at the same time.[11]

Many Americans mistakenly believe democracy makes politics consensual, in the same way membership in a country club or homeowners' association is consensual. Not so. While democracy is a blessing, it does not change the nature of the state. Governments possess a monopoly on the initiation of violence. Your local civic organization may kick you out if you don't pay your membership dues, but it won't send men with guns to your house. Try not paying your taxes and see if you get the same response. You'll find out the hard way civil society and government play by different rules.

Humans are social creatures, naturally prone to seek fellowship and form organizations to achieve their collective interests. Americans have always had a robust civic culture, which is why our nation is replete with clubs, friendly societies, and fraternities. Here's the crucial difference between society and state: No civil entity claims the right to use violence to settle its disputes. Sometimes they employ private security forces, but these are defensive. In contrast, government compels assent through coercion.

Nobody gets to say no to Uncle Sam. That's the price we pay for monopolizing law and order. Perhaps it's better to have a universal arbiter than every man deciding the rules for himself. But with a single decider comes a single point of vulnerability. Special interest groups, pursuing their own enrichment rather than the public welfare, have a strong incentive to capture the government. In a free state, wealth is created by honest labor. In a servile state, wealth is appropriated by legalized robbery. Libertarians are dedicated to preserving free institutions because we despise the idea of cronies oppressing the citizenry.

The Founding Fathers understood all this. They knew the American Revolution would be for naught if the political institutions they designed failed to protect the individual from the state. The culmination of their labors, the US Constitution, is a

---

11 James Madison. 1788. "The Structure of the Government Must Furnish the Proper Checks and Balances Between the Different Departments." *The New York Packet*, February 8.

masterwork of political engineering. Checks and balances, the separation of powers, federalism and the Bill of Rights all work together to prevent political predation. Unfortunately, we've ignored their wisdom. No constitution is perfectly self-enforcing. The only way to recover constitutionally limited government is to show crony-supporting politicians and bureaucrats the door.

Does this mean libertarians are always and everywhere opposed to government? Of course not! Libertarianism means forestalling the perils of government while realizing its potential. Going back to ancient Israel, the Western political tradition requires the state to protect the weak and innocent. Libertarianism fulfils this tradition. Furthermore, libertarians know there are many layers of government, each with its own sphere of competency. City hall is more accessible and responsive than Congress, and if push comes to shove, it's far easier to switch towns than countries.

Nevertheless, we must never romanticize government. Dreams of justice can easily become nightmares of oppression when backed by the irresistible force of the state. When we use politics to compel dissenters to subsidize our private interests, we trespass on human dignity and weaken civic cohesion. Persuasion, not force, is the standard of civilized men.

Government's value is instrumental: It depends on how well our public institutions protect our rights. But a government powerful enough to defend our rights is strong enough to violate them. The state never justifies itself. It's always accountable to its citizens, who retain the right to alter or abolish it. Libertarianism takes this insight to its natural conclusion: A free society embraces consent, not coercion.

Friedrich Nietzsche called the state the "coldest of all cold monsters."[12] Whatever else his errors, he was right about this. Political solutions to social problems aren't an exciting game, but a last resort. Free societies keep institutionalized violence to a minimum. Human flourishing itself is at stake.

---

12 Friedrich Nietzsche. 1896. *Thus Spake Zarathustra*. Tr. Alexander Tille. New York: Macmillan Publishers, p. 62.

8

FREE AND EQUAL:
Liberty and Natural Rights

As the renowned libertarian political philosopher Robert Nozick wrote, "Individuals have rights, and there are things no person or group may do to them."[13] On this rock libertarianism is built. Human dignity is central to the philosophy of liberty. Each of us has rights against aggression by others. These rights ground political justice. In a just society, every man receives his due. Before all else, he is due freedom.

If this sounds radical, good! It's meant to. It was radical in 1776, as well. Thomas Jefferson shook the world with the Declaration of Independence, which contains this immortal passage: "We hold these truths to be self-evident, that all men are created equal, that they are endowed, by their Creator, with certain unalienable Rights, that among these are Life, Liberty, and the pursuit of Happiness." Neither the prerogative of kings nor the demands of the masses justified the infringements of man's rights.

Murray Rothbard, one of the great libertarian theorists of the 20th century, explained the social implications of man's rights: "no man or group of men have the right to aggress against the person or property of anyone else."[14] This famous saying is known as the non-aggression principle. It rules out all coercion and fraud.

---

13 Robert Nozick. 1974. *Anarchy, State, and Utopia*. New York: Basic Books, p. ix.

14 Murray Rothbard. 1973. *For a New Liberty: The Libertarian Manifesto*. New York: Macmillan Publishers, p. 8.

Non-aggression is not the same as pacifism. Man has the right of self-defense, meaning the violent resistance of violence. But the *initiation* of force is impermissible.

In a free society, citizens respect the non-aggression principle in their dealings with each other. Just as important, society's public institutions respect it as well. This may be hard to imagine. Can we conceive of a government that doesn't use force to control individual behavior? The state always has some do-gooder scheme to foist on citizens, frequently with the best of intentions. But the desire to improve society doesn't justify using men as pawns. Adam Smith warned against the "man of system…so enamored with the supposed beauty of his own ideal plan of government, that he cannot suffer the smallest deviation from any part of it."[15] And to prevent such deviations, he's more than happy to dominate those who would rather be free.

Consent is the hallmark of libertarian social ethics. Disposing of peoples' property without their consent is theft. Disposing of peoples' bodies without their consent is assault. If a man wants to use another's property, he must first obtain the other's voluntary agreement. Here we see the libertarian approach to economics: Private property and free enterprise. Economic freedom is profoundly moral. It respects the dignity of persons and contributes to civilizational enrichment. Thanks to free enterprise, dire poverty is a thing of the past for the vast majority of the population. Even those of modest means live better than noblemen of centuries past. Imagine what we could achieve with even more economic freedom!

Would-be sophisticates frequently pooh-pooh libertarianism as "simplistic." They're wrong. Non-aggression is the heart of civilization. When we teach our children how to treat others, what do we say? Don't hurt people. Don't take what's theirs.[16]

---

15 Adam Smith. 1759. *The Theory of Moral Sentiments, or, An essay towards an analysis of the principles by which men naturally judge concerning the conduct and character, first of their neighbors, and afterwards of themselves.* London: Andrew Millar; Edinburgh: Alexander Kincaid and J. Bell.

16 Matt Kibbe. 2014. *Don't Hurt People and Don't Take Their Stuff: A Libertarian Manifesto.* William Morrow.

Call this "sandbox morality" if you like. It doesn't change the fact we expect it of everyone, both children and adults. Shouldn't we demand it of those who govern us, too? Libertarianism means refusing to base politics on a moral double-standard.

Another objection to libertarianism is its alleged inequality. Critics argue there's a tradeoff between freedom and fairness. Usually, they make this argument in the context of various social insurance schemes or similar redistributionist measures. But it's based on a false premise. Libertarianism is profoundly egalitarian. Every person has natural rights. Aggression is wrong, period. Government-sponsored redistribution is forced charity, meaning it isn't charity at all. Giving to those in need is noble. Coercing bystanders into government transfer programs isn't.

A society of true equals rests on non-aggression. There's no tradeoff between liberty and equality. They rise and fall together. Human persons are free and dignified peers by nature. Nobody has an inherent right to rule, and nobody has an inherent duty to serve. Again quoting Mr. Jefferson: "The mass of mankind has not been born with saddles on their backs, nor a favored few booted and spurred, ready to ride them legitimately, by the grace of God."[17] This is libertarianism. This is the Spirit of 1776. We've drifted far, but we can always correct course.

---

17 Thomas Jefferson. 1826. "Letter to Roger C. Weightman." June 24.

REASONS FOR RIGHTS:
Liberty and the Good Life

Natural rights are the foundation of a just government. Life, liberty, and property are non-negotiable. Our pursuit of happiness—meaning a life well-lived, not mere satisfaction or pleasure—requires the government to respect man's rights.

But where do these rights come from? The Declaration of Independence asserts that "all men" are "endowed by their Creator" with rights. Many Founders believed in a divine sanction for each person's moral entitlements. To them, respecting natural rights meant honoring God, the source of human dignity. We have a duty to protect rights because we have a duty to obey God.

However, natural rights are not a specifically religious concept. Even those who don't believe in God understand the natural equality of men, also proclaimed in the Declaration. Because human persons are moral equals, we must regard our fellows as ends in themselves. When we trample on the rights of others, we subordinate them to our own ends. It's wrong to treat people like tools. A human being is not an instrument to be manipulated by his presumed betters. Equal personhood means equal dignity, which establishes rights as a universal principle.

Natural rights deserve protection for reasons other than duty. Consequences matter, too. "Every tree is known by its fruit," Jesus of Nazareth said. For example, societies that value life, liberty, and property are wealthier, healthier, and more socially equal than societies that don't. A rights-respecting society is a free society, in which human ingenuity can best solve important social problems. Creativity requires freedom because creativity can't function under coercion.

The greatest institution for harnessing ingenuity is the free market. Once upon a time, all of humanity was wretchedly poor. Now, thanks to the power of markets, we enjoy living standards unimaginable to our ancestors. On average, an American earns about $63,000 per year. That's roughly $170 per day. In comparison, it wasn't that long ago that everyone but aristocrats had to live on less than $2 per day. This enrichment would've been impossible without market-supported innovation, which in turn requires private property and the rule of law. Free markets are the extension into the economic sphere of man's natural rights.

If duty is too abstract a concept for you, an 85-fold increase in living standards is a pretty good reason to defend natural rights! Life, liberty, and property deliver the goods, plain and simple.

Protecting rights also helps us become better people. We have to work at performing our duties. Good consequences don't happen by themselves; we have to create them. Our ability to build worthy lives for ourselves, our families, and our communities depends on good ethical habits, which help us bear the weight of duty and strive for great achievements. In the Western philosophical tradition, we call these ethical habits *virtues*. A virtuous person is someone who has exercised his moral muscles, over and over again. You become a good man the same way you become good at free throws or the piano: Practice, practice, practice.

Those philosophers who believe "statecraft is soulcraft" want to use politics to make men good. But the most the government can do is make us free, because freedom is a prerequisite for virtue. Coerced virtue is a contradiction in terms. A soldier who fights only when compelled by his commanding officer isn't courageous. A citizen who gives to the poor only when compelled by a bureaucrat isn't charitable. Natural rights promote virtue by creating the social conditions necessary for people to flourish. Citizens protected against force and fraud are free to work on the most important project of all: Themselves.

Duty, consequences, and virtue point to a common truth: Natural rights are woven into the fabric of reality. True justice requires life, liberty, and property.

THE LIMITS OF LAW:
Why Government Shouldn't Force Us to be Good

"You can't legislate morality," the old saying goes. In a narrow sense, this is wrong. All legislation rests on some moral principle. The minute you use the word "ought" in the sentence "The government ought..." you've entered prescriptive territory. Viewed this way, the *only* thing you can legislate is morality!

But the old saying is right if we interpret it broadly. Here's what it really means: Governments can't force us to be good. It just doesn't work. While the government should make demands on us only if they are moral, it doesn't follow that everything moral must be mandatory, nor everything immoral prohibited. Such a society would be a totalitarian nightmare. Government's job is to serve as the public's protector, not its conscience.

Law is not morality. Many immoral things should not be illegal. In a free society, the state doesn't punish all vice, nor does it reward all virtue. Liberty means limiting government to its core functions: Protecting citizens from force and fraud.

It's always tempting to use politics to impose our vision of the Good Society on everyone else. Why should we tolerate stubborn, unpatriotic individuals standing in the way of justice? But this way of thinking is dangerous. Remember, you probably seem like a stubborn, unpatriotic individual to those who disagree with you about what the Good Society looks like! If the domain of politics becomes all of morality, we've essentially declared a war of all against all. Now it's a race to capture the government. Winners get to reward their friends and punish their enemies. If the stakes of politics are this high, the chances of us living together in peace are slim.

Here's another problem with the "statecraft as soulcraft" philosophy. History shows us plenty of examples where governments tried to force morality on the public, only for it to backfire. Exhibit A in the United States is alcohol prohibition. The Eighteenth Amendment was a disaster. People didn't stop drinking. Instead, the production and consumption of alcohol moved into black markets. Various mob organizations, already skilled at using violence to enrich themselves, happily took up the work of bootlegging. A large fraction of the public viewed prohibition as an imposition by moral busybodies. Citizens scorned the dignity of law itself. In short, prohibition failed. Whatever the problems caused by drinking, the government's cure was worse than the disease. Thank goodness for the Twenty-First Amendment!

Sadly, we never really learned the lesson of prohibition. The War on Drugs is making the same mistakes in bigger, more expensive ways. Many people think drug use is immoral. They have a case. But it doesn't follow that drugs should be illegal. The predictable result of the War on Drugs is lucrative black markets controlled by murderous cartels. The drugs themselves become more potent, and hence more dangerous. Those trapped in addiction often can't seek help. Society is poorer, sicker, and more violent due to the War on Drugs, all because too many citizens overlooked the difference between morality and law.

There are some immoral things the government should prohibit, of course. Murder, assault, theft, and abuse come easily to mind. The whole point of government is to crack down on these horrid acts. Why doesn't this run afoul of the "law isn't morality" maxim? Remember, what makes a government a government is its monopoly on legitimized initiatory violence. Only Uncle Sam gets to strike first. We put up with this big, scary entity on the condition it uses its power to keep the peace. Government should behave like a referee, not like a player. And it certainly shouldn't penalize some players because it thinks other players ought to win.

"Everything I dislike should be banned!" is the philosophy of a petulant child, not a self-governing adult. Maturity means living in harmony with your neighbors, even if you disapprove of their behavior. This isn't an endorsement of moral subjectivism. Some things really are good and others bad. But for the sake of political harmony, as well as our own virtue, we must not use coercion to stamp out vice. Only if we stifle our urge to boss other people around can we maintain a free society.

CAN A CHRISTIAN BE A LIBERTARIAN?

"Do not put your trust in princes, in mortal men who have no power to save." Ps. 146:3

"The kings of the Gentiles exercise lordship over them, and those in authority over them are called benefactors. But not so with you. Rather, let the greatest among you become as the youngest, and the leader as one who serves." Lk. 22:25-26

A liberty-first approach to politics requires certain moral assumptions. Those assumptions come from our beliefs about human dignity and what we owe our neighbors and communities. Are these beliefs compatible with Christianity? Although religiosity is declining in America, about two-thirds of the population still identifies as Christian. This means the relationship between Christianity and libertarianism is very important.

While it's blasphemous to identify Christianity with partisan agendas, Christ's teachings do have political implications. Politics is about how we arrange our communal affairs, which depends on our values. Jesus had some things to say about values! How well do they mesh with libertarianism?

Reasonably well, I'd say. Christianity and libertarianism both entail a healthy skepticism of power, especially political power.

As Fr. Alexander Schmemann writes, the state is "limited by its very nature…[and] is a blessing only to the extent that it serves God's plan for man."[18] I don't think libertarianism is a uniquely Christian approach to politics. But I do think there's a path from the Christian understanding of human dignity to the libertarian imperative of minimal government. In fact, libertarianism as a philosophy never would have arisen except in a society already deeply infused with Christian ethical principles.

Government isn't the only powerful entity in society. What makes it uniquely worrying? Remember, the problem with government is not *what* it does, but *how* it does it. The essence of government is force. Of all society's institutions, only government claims the right to inflict grievous bodily harm, perhaps even death, on those who defy it. This power is how government gets away with many of its unjust acts. These include, in collaboration with corporate elites, economic exploitation. Christianity condemns these injustices. Libertarianism does, too.

Entire libraries could be written on Christians' uncomfortable relationship with political power. I limit myself to two Biblical examples here. Each illustrates the moral perils of government.

The first is from the Old Testament. 1 Samuel 8 recounts the origins of Israel's monarchy. The Israelites reject God's kingship and demand a human king to lead them in battle against the Gentiles. Samuel warns the people about the consequences of their choice:

He will take the best of your fields and vineyards and olive groves and give them to his attendants. He will take a tenth of your grain and of your vintage and give it to his officials and attendants. Your male and female servants and the best of your cattle and donkeys he will take for his own use. He will take a tenth of your flocks, and you yourselves will become his slaves.

---

18 Alexander Schmemann. 1997. *The Historical Raod of Eastern Orthodoxy.* Crestwood, NY: St Vladimirs Seminary Press.

Even this account is not a total rejection of politics. God grants the request. Yet Scripture is clearly showing us how political and economic exploitation are entwined. Be careful what you wish for!

The second is from the New Testament. After His baptism but before His public ministry, Christ is driven by the Holy Spirit into the wilderness, where He is tempted by the devil. In St. Matthew's (4:1-11) account, Christ's final temptation is earthly political authority. Satan offers Christ "all the kingdoms of the world and their glory" if Christ will worship him. This presumes the power is Satan's to give. St. Luke's (4:1-13) version is even more explicit: Authority over the kingdoms "has been delivered to me, and I will give it to whom I will," boasts the Adversary. Importantly, in neither account does Christ dispute the devil's authority over the kingdoms. Later in the New Testament, St. Paul makes similar points, linking earthly political power with demonic fraternization (1 Cor. 2:8; Eph. 6:12). This isn't a road Christians should be eager to follow.

Israel wanted an earthly king rather than God. Satan wanted to be king instead of God. Ultimately, both errors are the same. There is only one King: YHWH Sabaoth, Lord of Hosts. Whenever we try to place anyone or anything besides God at the center of our lives, including our public life, we commit idolatry. Lest we Christians get too big for our britches, we also commit this sin. Politicized Christianity is ubiquitous in America. This is an abomination. Jesus is not a capitalist nor a socialist. Jesus is not a conservative nor a liberal. Jesus is not a Republican nor a Democrat. Jesus is "the Christ, the Son of the Living God." (Mt. 16:16). The only true Christian polity is the Church. In her is the fullness of Christ's kingly reign.

No secular ideology, including libertarianism, fully embodies Christianity's public witness. Christ tells us to give Caesar his due (Mt. 22:21). St. Paul, inspired by the Holy Spirit, commands us to be obedient and peaceful towards government (Rom. 13:1-7). For us Americans, reared on the romance of revolution, these are hard teachings! Yet they are God's commands. We must follow them.

Libertarianism becomes another kind of political idolatry if taken too far. Whether pro-government or anti-government, any philosophy that reifies politics is dangerous. Again quoting Fr. Schmemann, "The state is only Christian to the extent that it does not claim to be everything for man–to define his whole life–but enables him to be a member of another community, another reality, which is alien to the state although not hostile to it."[19]

Libertarianism is not the "correct" Christian theory of politics. But it's perfectly legitimate for Christians to adopt libertarian political stances. As long as government operates through violence, we who bear the image of God should regard it warily.

19 Ibid., p. 152.

FREE ENTERPRISE, NOT CAPITALISM

Political freedom and economic freedom go hand-in-hand. Without economic freedom, political freedom is useless. You may get a vote, but the state ultimately dictates your life and livelihood. Without political freedom, economic freedom is an illusion. Oligarchs dominate society and your "right" to property is merely a government dispensation. Freedom is a package deal. We need both kinds to flourish.

Libertarians vigorously defend political and economic freedom. Properly ordered, markets and government reinforce each other. They have common institutional roots in private property, freedom of contract, and the rule of law. This political-economic model is called *free enterprise*.

Capitalism is not the same as free enterprise. We commonly use "capitalism" to mean "private ownership of the means of production." This is misguided. We need to take a broader historical perspective. In reality, capitalism looks quite different from free enterprise. The former is ripe with cronyism. It's the latter we should fight for.

Here's the essential difference between capitalism and free enterprise. Capitalism is pro-business. Its slogan is, "What's good for Wall Street is good for America." But free enterprise is pro-market. Its slogan is, "Property rights for all, special privileges for none." For defenders of liberty and equality, free enterprise is clearly superior.

The problem with capitalism is it privatizes benefits while socializing costs. Private property is necessary for freedom, but not sufficient. Capitalists rig the game so that they keep their profits while forcing taxpayers to cover their losses. This is both economically harmful and socially unjust. We saw the pernicious side of capitalism following the financial crisis of 2008. Wall Street got a bailout. Main Street paid the tab.

Historically, the development of several important markets, including financial markets, depended on an alliance between economic elites and political elites. Powerful bankers and merchants comprised the economic elite; powerful aristocrats and bureaucrats comprised the political elite. They struck bargains that enriched themselves at the expense of the public. Economic elites supplied capital; political elites supplied government privileges. While they reaped immense wealth, the public bore the costs.

Adam Smith, the godfather of modern economics, understood the difference between free enterprise and capitalism. His *Wealth of Nations*, published the same year America declared its independence, extolled the benefits of free enterprise. Given a level economic playing field and genuine competition, private property is a great boon to national wealth. But political and economic elites constantly try to quash free enterprise. "People of the same trade seldom meet together, even for merriment and diversion, but the conversation ends in a conspiracy against the public," Smith warned.[20] His insight is timeless.

Capitalism vs. free enterprise is an important theme in U.S. history. It goes back to the Founding of the country. During the early years of the Republic, supporters of capitalism and supporters of free enterprise lined up on opposite sides of the ball. The capitalist party wanted a strong central government, a permanent national debt, and protective tariffs. The free enterprise party wanted strong local governments, the swift retirement of national debt, and free trade. Despite occasional setbacks, the capitalists won.

---

20 Adam Smith. 1776. *The Nature and Causes of the Wealth of Nations*. London: W. Strahan and T. Cadell. Vol I, p. 160.

Let's do a little myth-busting. The conventional wisdom about big businesses hating regulations and taxes is wrong. In fact, big businesses love these things. They know they can cope with these burdens much more easily than their smaller, nimbler competitors. Regulation and taxes don't promote competition. They stifle competition. If we want to restore free enterprise, we need to reform our byzantine web of economic restrictions. Let people produce and trade freely. Free enterprise means everyone has a right to seek their fortune without big business or big government blocking the way.

When Facebook was small and scrappy, CEO Mark Zuckerberg vigorously defended free expression. Now that Facebook is large and dominant, Zuckerberg appears before Congress to ask for government regulation of social media. This is capitalism in a nutshell. Americans are tired of the wealthy and powerful exempting themselves from the rules the rest of us must follow. We need a renewed push for free enterprise. Libertarians are leading the charge.

FREEDOM AND ORDER

"Order is the first need of the commonwealth," wrote Russell Kirk, the great scholar of Anglo-American conservatism. Without order, "it is not possible for us to live in peace with one another."[21] A good society has a high degree of order. But it also, libertarians insist, has a high degree of freedom. Is there a tradeoff here? Must we sacrifice freedom to secure order?

Perhaps in dire circumstances, such as a war for national survival, we would face this painful choice. But in surprisingly many cases, freedom and order reinforce each other. One of the most important discoveries of modern social science is that *freedom is orderly.* Liberty is a necessary component of social harmony.

Hierarchy is the most familiar kind of order. What makes businesses function efficiently? How do militaries carry out precise operations? The answer in both cases is the same: There's somebody issuing commands. Well-regulated social groups frequently have a regulator.

But not always. In fact, more expansive forms of order could not exist if we tried to run the country like a barracks. Social harmony is the unintended result of innumerable free human choices. This is called *spontaneous order*—in the words of the Scottish Enlightenment philosopher Adam Ferguson, "the result of human action, but not the execution of any human design."[22]

---

21 Russell Kirk. 1974. *Roots of American Order.* Open Court Publishing Company.
22 Adam Ferguson. 1767. *An Essay on the History of Civil Society.* Boulter Grierson.

Markets are the classic example of spontaneous order. Every week, thousands of supermarkets across the nation put about as much milk on their shelves as customers want to buy. Shortages and surpluses are rare. Yet nobody calls the supermarket beforehand to reserve a gallon of milk. We show up assuming the milk will be there, and most of the time we're right. You can thank the market price system, the most sophisticated communications network ever devised by man, for this small miracle and millions like it.

If the price of milk were too high, customers would purchase less than the supermarket wanted to sell. If the price of milk were too low, the supermarket would sell less than customers wanted to buy. Only when the price is right is there a balance between supply and demand. Decentralized coordination through commercial transactions is how we all get milk, as well as iPhones, Hawaiian vacations, and blockbuster movies. Markets are far too complex to plan from the top-down. Coordination happens spontaneously from the bottom-up.

All well and good, the liberty-skeptics reply, but markets can only exist in a society that's already orderly. Commerce presupposes property rights and the rule of law, forms of order that must be imposed by the government. Without these prerequisites, we couldn't sustain an advanced division of labor. Freedom still depends on order.

There's something to this objection, but less than the liberty skeptics think. Historically, commerce and law grew up together. For example, going back to the Middle Ages, international traders used a noncompulsory legal system to resolve their disputes. Called the *lex mercatoria*, or "law merchant," its precedents were based on specialist judges' decisions in voluntary proceedings. Ornery traders who decided to ignore the rulings were not actively punished. However, their fellow merchants would ostracize them. The prospect of losing future business, and hence profits, gave everyone an incentive to play nice.

Even today, most international trade is privately governed. This shouldn't surprise us: Its global character means no national court has clear jurisdiction. Despite these anarchic conditions, commerce across national boundaries has been orderly for centuries. Even great wars do not completely shut it down. Spontaneous order can work for the "rules of the game," too.

Libertarians don't dispute the need for order. We simply deny it extends from the barrel of a gun. David Friedman, a libertarian economist and legal theorist, put it best: "Indeed, the direct use of force is so poor a solution to the problem of limited resources and diverse ends that it is rarely employed save by small children and great nations."[23] The ultimate form of disorder is not anarchy, but tyranny.

---

23 David D. Friedman. 2001. *Law's Order: What Economics Has to Do with Law and Why It Matters*. Princeton University Press.

THE CONSTITUTION IS DEAD.
LONG LIVE THE CONSTITUTION!

The Constitution of the United States is not a strictly libertarian document. It empowers the national government to protect citizens' natural rights, which is appropriate. However, it also gives Uncle Sam a wide berth to "promote the general welfare,"[24] which makes libertarians uneasy. Lovers of liberty point out that one man's "general welfare" is another man's burdensome tax bill. Political elites tend to interpret the scope of their powers in ways that benefit themselves at the expense of the public.

In our national memory, the Constitution represents a triumph of limited government. But this romantic story doesn't fit the facts. The Constitution was a deliberate attempt to strengthen government by expanding its powers. The Federalists, chafing under the Articles of Confederation, thought we needed a robust, independent executive and much more legislative leeway. They were concerned more with national greatness and high statecraft than liberty. Devotees of power such as Alexander Hamilton and Robert Morris would likely be aghast at what Washington, DC has become. But they set in motion the forces that got us here.

The Bill of Rights provides some help. Undoubtedly the Constitution's first ten amendments have prevented some egregious

---

24 While this is not a specific grant of power, it does suggest a troubling broad mandate for public coercion.

abuses of power. But not enough. Even here there was a missed opportunity—or rather, a clever political plan. The 10th Amendment asserts that powers not delegated to the national government remain with state governments or the citizens themselves. But this obvious nod to federalism is less helpful than it looks. The Framers deliberately omitted the word "expressly" from the 10th Amendment, a word that featured prominently in Article II of the Articles of Confederation. There's a world of difference between "expressly delegated" and "delegated." The latter leaves far more room for interpretation, which ambitious political operatives often use to expand government power, but never to limit it.

In short, while the Constitution establishes limited and lawful government, it does not establish libertarian government. But until we persuade the public about the value of liberty, it's the only game in town. When facing a government run amok, pushing for Constitutional fidelity is itself a libertarian project. We can quibble about Congress's money-creating and taxing powers later. Right now, the goal is getting back to the user's manual.

While there are a range of plausible interpretations of the Constitution, the words in the text can only be stretched so far. The plain fact of the matter is much of what the federal government does today is unconstitutional, and therefore illegal. Curbing these abuses won't yield a libertarian government. But we'll get much closer than by doing anything else. Let's not fall into the familiar libertarian trap of making the perfect the enemy of the good.

Today's biggest threats to liberty can be stymied by rolling back the national government. For example, the administrative state—consisting of career bureaucrats who write their own rules and force them on the public—is clearly a Constitutional abomination. It's not about the content of the rules; it's about where the rules come from. Libertarians must insist that legislation come from Congress, and nowhere else. If a proposed rule can't make it through Congress, that means the public is sufficiently divided on the issue that the right action is inaction, until dialogue and persuasion have time to work.

Going through Congress is sometimes the libertarian answer.

But not always. While we need to bolster the legislature against the executive branch, we also must keep the legislature within its proper bounds. That means recognizing the limits to the various Article 1 powers. For example, the authority "to regulate commerce...among the several states" does not mean elected officials can micromanage the nation's business affairs. Incredibly, Congress has used this clause to justify its regulation of farmers growing wheat for their own consumption, as well as the production and sale of milk solely within a state. The reason? These activities *hypothetically* could affect trade between states! The clause isn't really that elastic, of course. Stretching things this far is clearly absurd.

Finally, the executive branch needs to be taken down a peg or two. In addition to curbing the administrative agencies, we need much stricter limits on presidential power. Executive orders have become de facto legislation. That's unconstitutional. The president now has near-unlimited ability to conduct military operations without a declaration of war from Congress. That's unconstitutional. If you want to know why the stakes of presidential elections have gotten so high, look no further than presidents' habitual disregard of the Constitution.

There's no viable path to political change that doesn't operate within the Constitution. Libertarians should make their peace with an imperfect charter for the sake of a more perfect union. Partisans of the left and right ignore the rules when it's inconvenient, but we cannot do likewise. The rule of law is a fundamental libertarian value, and we lose more than we gain when we betray our principles. The time is ripe for Constitutional renewal. Libertarians should sound the call loud and clear.

PART III

AMERICAN LIBERTY IN THE 21ST CENTURY

KEEP GOVERNMENT SMALL AND LOCAL

At the beginning of the 20th century, government at all levels consumed about 10 percent of the national income. State and local governments used up twice as much as the federal government. Today, the situation is vastly different. The public sector devours 30 percent of the national income, with the federal government out-consuming state and local governments roughly two to one. These are the most important political trends of the last 100 years: A massive increase in the overall size of government combined with a reversal in the layer of government with the biggest footprint.

Defenders of ordered liberty should regard these changes warily. Freedom and order thrive when government is strictly limited. Yet if the public sector must expand to meet some new challenge, it should happen at the smallest scale possible. These pillars of political wisdom have been largely ignored since the Progressive era. An uncontrolled, unaccountable, irresponsible government is the result.

Pollsters will tell you Americans don't much care for these "procedural" niceties. So long as the economy is strong at home and the military isn't getting whipped abroad, voters are supposedly unconcerned about the scale and scope of government. Let's hope this sleepy indifference to federalist fundamentals doesn't last. Outcomes matter. But process matters, too—or else America's Constitutional tradition is bunk.

Remember what we discussed before? "The only winning move is not to play."[25] The solution isn't feeding Leviathan different prey. It's shackling Leviathan! Until we radically downsize the government, reallocating to states and municipalities those few activities that are truly in the public interest, we'll never experience the civic flourishing that is ours by right.

Washington, DC shouldn't do anything that can be accomplished at the state or local level. In our federal system, the primary responsibility of the federal government is foreign policy. It's proper to keep the armed forces in fit-fighting shape, as well as maintain a diplomatic corps capable of engaging other nations responsibly. There are some national-level domestic duties, of course. The court system is important. Basic infrastructure is justifiable. A case can be made for national parks and the space program. Reasonable people can disagree about specific policies. Nevertheless, for most of what Uncle Sam does, the case for a national response is weak.

But what about environmental protections? A simple pollution tax could get the incentives right. No need for mammoth entities like the Department of Energy or the Environmental Protection Agency, which have predictably devolved into dispensers of political favors. But what about the social safety net? We can't give up on Social Security and Medicare! Spoiler alert: We already have. The Committee for a Responsible Federal Budget predicts the Medicare Hospital Insurance Fund will be insolvent by 2028, and Social Security in its entirety by 2035. These programs were always accounting gimmicks used to purchase votes with future tax dollars that never materialized. Let's just be honest and get Uncle Sam out of the health care and retirement care businesses. It's lousy at these things.

Sadly, state and local officials are some of the biggest opponents of responsible government. Many governors thunder about the importance of federalism when they're on the campaign trail. Yet once cozily ensconced in office, they're happy to take as much

---

25 John Badham. 1983. *WarGames*. United Artists and Sherwood Productions.

Beltway loot as they can get their hands on, because it lets them dispense goodies to their political allies. Remember, "He who pays the piper calls the tune." You can't defend local government if you're attached to the Washington cash spigot. There's a reason the Founders paid such careful attention to government's fiscal prerogatives. The power of the purse is the power to create dependency. But only independent layers of government can protect citizens from Imperial City overreach.

The perpetual struggle between Team Red and Team Blue for control over the national government is largely a distraction. As long as state and local authorities remain junior partners, the public sector will remain institutionally irresponsible. The American system is built on federalism for a reason. The whole project is designed to empower the protective and productive functions of government while forestalling its predatory potentials. Until and unless a critical mass of politicians is willing to answer 95 percent of press questions with, "That's a matter for state and local governments, so it's none of my business," the public sector will become ever more expensive yet less effective.

LOCAL LIBERTY:
Freedom at the State Level

I've had lots to say about the history of libertarianism and its relationship to the American political tradition. But I haven't spent much time on specific libertarian policy reforms. It's time to take a closer look at how freedom can help us flourish

However, we won't go straight to federal policy. It's true Washington is in dire need of a libertarian makeover. But there's plenty that can and should be done at the state level. State governments are well-positioned to serve as laboratories of liberty. We can experiment with different reforms to see what works and what doesn't. This is why libertarians are so fond of federalism: Decentralization makes for happier, healthier politics.

Right here in Texas, two policies have standout prospects: School choice and sound budgeting. In fact, all states could benefit from these policies, but conditions in Texas are particularly ripe for these reforms. A libertarian agenda on education and spending can make a huge difference in families' wellbeing.

Let's start with K-12 education. Texas spends just shy of $10,000 per student per year. This is roughly equal to average private school tuition in the state. Admittedly, public and private schooling are complex bundles of goods and services that defy exact comparisons. The fact remains that there's no *financial* obstacle to ensuring every young Texan receives a quality education.

Public education funding is incredibly complex. Actual spending per student is determined by school districts and public charter schools, who receive funds from one of two "holding tank" accounts. Those resources in turn come from the state general fund, dedicated taxes, and a publicly owned investment portfolio. Along the way, funds are augmented or diminished according to several difficult-to-understand formulas, many of which result from partisan agendas in Austin.

What if, instead of running this highly inefficient gauntlet, we gave the money directly to families? Imagine we offered every family an Education Savings Account, into which those funds were deposited. Parents could spend the money on tuition, books, tutoring, extracurriculars, and even homeschooling. The requirement in the Texas Constitution that the Legislature support the "general diffusion of knowledge" doesn't require the government to *produce* education. It only must *fund* education.

From 2020 to 2021, seventeen states experimented with or inaugurated school choice programs. COVID-19 and school closures gave parents across the country an up-close look at the seedy underbelly of public education. They didn't like what they saw, which is why education freedom is such a hot issue. It's time for Texas to take its rightful place among the vanguard of school reform movements by funding students, not systems. Parents should control their children's' education dollars. That's a clear win for both liberty and the common good.

As for sound budgeting, the argument is simple: Every dollar spent in Austin is a dollar taken from households, businesses, or civic organizations. While some of those outlays go to important public infrastructure, far too much ends up in the pockets of political cronies. We need to control overall spending so the communities in which we live and work can thrive. Texas has decent fiscal rules, such as balanced budget requirements and spending limits based on personal income growth. But we shouldn't settle for decent when excellence is within reach.

Public spending hikes should be capped at population growth plus inflation. In other words, resources used per resident by the government should remain constant. Austin spends about $4,500 per capita each year. There's no reason for this to get bigger, other than to keep up with the dollar's diminished purchasing power. We spend plenty already. Our problem now is getting the most bang for our buck.

Obviously, the composition of public spending matters. But so does the top-line figure. A libertarian approach to state fiscal policy ensures the government has enough to perform its essential duties, but no more. Anything greater imposes undue hardships on families. There's only one successful welfare program over the long term: Economic growth. We need free enterprise to create a rising tide of prosperity, which requires public authorities to stay in their lanes. Keeping government spending under control enables public prudence and private initiative to complement each other.

Freedom enables flourishing. That's why libertarianism puts liberty front and center, even at the state level. You can't have good government without respecting citizens' rights. The whole point of pro-liberty reforms is giving people more control over their own lives. School choice restores parents' rights to decide what kind of education is right for their children. Budget limits strengthen citizens' ability to discipline and control their government. Let's put libertarianism to work right here at home.

NATIONAL ECONOMY POLICY AND LIBERTY

Many Americans believe the government has a responsibility to fight recessions. They shouldn't. Politicians and bureaucrats are lousy at stabilizing markets. Their nostrums usually do more harm than good.

Economics textbooks will tell you there are two ways the government can smooth out the business cycle. The first is fiscal policy. By ratcheting up spending, Congress and the president can give the economy a shot in the arm. The second is monetary policy. The Federal Reserve, our nation's central bank, can meet extraordinary liquidity demand by printing new money. What the textbooks rarely say—and this should be front and center—is that the former rarely works, and the latter only works under specific conditions.

Let's start with fiscal policy. For government spending to jolt the economy, it must increase aggregate demand (total spending on goods and services). But oftentimes, if Uncle Sam consumes more, someone else must consume less. Public spending crowds out private spending. When this happens, fiscal policy doesn't create jobs or boost incomes. It just shuffles around existing jobs and incomes.

But let's be charitable and assume fiscal policy can help. There's an even bigger problem: Effective fiscal policy must be timely, targeted, and temporary. *Timely* means the spending package has to pass Congress and get the president's signature before markets improve on their own. *Targeted* means spending should focus on those sectors of the economy suffering the most. And *temporary* means spending must fall once the economy recovers, or else we might overshoot the recovery.

Given everything you know about politics, how likely is it that emergency spending will satisfy these three criteria? Do you trust elected officials to decide quickly, spend responsibly, and voluntarily turn off the spigot once the economy steadies?

I'll wait for you to finish laughing.

Now we turn to monetary policy. Unlike spending, printing money is pretty good at expanding aggregate demand. When the Fed purchases assets, such as government bonds, it credits its counterparty's bank account with newly created money. In economics jargon, the Fed meets an increase in money demand by expanding the money supply. This can prevent a downturn if it's done right. Since the Fed has a legal monopoly on the monetary base (the narrowest measure of the money supply, consisting of bank deposits held at the Fed and physical currency), it's the only game in town when there's a flight from securities to dollars.

But don't put too much trust in central bankers. They mess up all the time. To stabilize markets, the monetary expansion must be sized just right. Guess what happens if it's too big? That's right, inflation! During 2022, the U.S. economy experienced its strongest price pressures in 40 years. Perhaps the Fed's doubling of the monetary base from Spring 2020 to Fall 2021 had something to do with that. Milton Friedman was right after all: "A more rapid increase in the quantity of money than in output" is a predictable recipe for inflation.

This isn't the only kind of money mischief. Expanding the money supply sometimes lowers interest rates. All else being equal, the more liquidity flowing through capital markets, the lower the price of capital, which is interest. When interest rates fall due to a genuine increase in savings, all well and good. The lower price of capital signals to investors that loanable funds are more abundant. But what happens when interest rates fall only because of the Fed's "funny money" effect? Investors are fooled into thinking capital is more abundant than it really is. As a result, they undertake many unsustainable projects. Boom inevitably turns to bust. If this sounds familiar, it's because this happened with the 2008 subprime mortgage crisis. We built too many houses, and securitized too many mortgages, because the Fed kept interest rates too low for too long from 2003-5.

In truth, we don't need a central bank at all. A free market for money and finance works just as well as for pizza, laptops, and sportscoats. As long as we're stuck with the Fed, we must bind its hands with a strict rule. Like medicine, the first rule of monetary policy is not doing harm. No inflationary expansions. No misleading interest rates. Congress can and should rein in the Fed by ordering the central bank to keep the dollar's value steady.

Besides economic damage, there's another pernicious effect of government intervention: We become less free. Whenever the economic outlook sours, the government plots to spend, regulate, and print more money. Markets become increasingly dependent on government largesse. American financial markets, once the envy of the world, have become addicted to spending splurges and easy credit. Political patronage props up entire industries. Private property and voluntary contract are supposed to safeguard our independence and livelihoods. Yet under the guise of stabilization policy, Washington turns these instruments of liberty into tools of servility.

Political planning and technocratic tinkering render markets less stable, not more. With each passing crisis (likely created by government in the first place) the national debt and the Fed's balance sheet grow ever-larger. Our nation would be freer and richer if Uncle Sam stopped trying to micromanage the economy.

HEALTHCARE AND LIBERTY

Healthcare is hotly debated in contemporary politics. What role should government play in the provision of medical services? Many people believe healthcare is a human right. As such, the government should make it available to the public free of charge. This sounds compassionate and humane. It's not. The more we examine proposals for government-funded medicine—let alone government-run medicine—the less attractive it becomes.

Be very careful before you declare something a human right. All rights come with obligations. When the Founding Fathers proclaimed a natural right to life, they meant a right not to be murdered. We have a negative obligation to refrain from harming our neighbors. But a right to health care creates a positive obligation, which necessarily means a right to compel doctors, nurses, pharmacists, and a host of other medical professionals to work for free. But is it just to treat these competent, well-trained, hardworking professionals as exploitable tools? (You can't avoid this by having the government compensate them; the money must come from somewhere, meaning someone will have their property forcibly taken.) Human dignity requires us to treat others not as means to an end, but as ends in themselves. Yet positive rights, such as the "right" to healthcare, reduce people to cogs in a machine.

The public demands more government involvement in healthcare because the industry appears dysfunctional. But misguided government policy is the main reason for healthcare problems in the first place. Just look at insurance. In a healthy market, insurance providers would offer a variety of packages with different premiums and coverage levels. Some would cover only catastrophic medical emergencies. Others would cover mundane treatments as well, with higher premiums to account for the higher expected expenditures. Households could pick the packages that worked best for them, based on their risk preferences and ability to pay. Unfortunately, existing insurance markets don't look anything like this. The government often mandates "cadillac" insurance packages, depriving consumers of lower-cost options. The market is heavily distorted by taxes and subsidies. Competition across state lines is restricted. This isn't anywhere close to free enterprise.

We see similar problems in the prices for actual medical care.[26] Over the past 20 years, medical services have gotten more than 100 percent more expensive. Hospital services specifically are almost 200 percent more expensive. Over the same period, prices in general increased 50 percent, meaning healthcare is becoming much less affordable in inflation-adjusted terms. The problem here is that healthcare is priceless.[27] I mean that literally: Healthcare consumers almost never confront a market price. Consumers only pay 10 percent of healthcare expenditures out of pocket. Roughly 90 percent are paid by third parties—not only private insurance, but Medicare, Medicaid, the Department of Veterans Affairs, and other entities. Big government made this mess.

Compare this to the prices of cosmetic procedures, which are usually not covered by third parties. Over the past 20 years, most common procedures have increased in price, but less than prices in general. These procedures are getting more affordable on an inflation-adjusted basis. The difference is consumers have much stronger incentives to spend wisely since nobody else is footing

---

26 Mark J. Perry. 2018. "What Economic Lessons About Health Care Costs Can We Learn from the Competitive Market for Cosmetic Procedures?" AEIdeas, March 30.

27 Alexander William Salter. 2020. "Salter: Your health care is priceless; that's a big problem." *Lubbock Avalanche-Journal*, March 15.

the bill. Importantly, cosmetic procedures are not categorically different from other procedures. They all require highly trained doctors, specialized tools, and other costly equipment. Yet because the cosmetic market is much freer of government interference, we get increasing affordability. Steady improvements in technology and productivity make (inflation-adjusted) prices go down. There's no reason health services in general should defy this trend. The only thing standing in the way is the government's misguided policies.

Healthcare is essential for human wellbeing. We should try to make it as widely available as possible. But good intentions aren't enough. We need strategies that work. Sadly, government involvement in healthcare has been a disaster for both freedom and efficiency. The solution is to remove as many roadblocks to market competition as possible. Second-best options, such as expanding tax-free health savings accounts, might also be a good idea. Such policies are not strictly libertarian, but they're much more just and effective than what we've got now.

19

END THE ENTITLEMENT STATE

The entitlement state is on its last legs. Based on recent estimates, the Social Security trust fund will run out in 2037. Medicare's Part A trust fund, which covers hospital insurance, will deplete in 2028. Insolvency forces sudden and painful across-the-board benefit cuts: 20 percent to Social Security and 10 percent to Medicare Part A. Libertarians have warned about the unsustainability of these programs for decades. Few listened. Soon, everybody will have to listen.

Creating these programs in the first place was a mistake. The welfare state, a 19th century Prussian invention, has no place in the land of the free. A combination of political cynicism and elitist paternalism brought it to our shores. We're worse off for it. Expansive federal entitlements crowd out private-sector and civil-society responses, harming the very people the programs were intended to help. Even more worryingly, they make citizens dependent on government.

The only accomplishment of America's entitlement state is permanent fiscal profligacy. Washington is currently in the red somewhere between $50 trillion and $200 trillion (!) because of these programs. That's in addition to our official national debt of roughly $30 trillion. The combination of unfunded entitlement liabilities and debt erodes the independence on which our national freedom depends. The Founders would weep.

There's no realistic prospect to save these programs. Citizens simply won't tolerate the tax rates necessary to fund them. That's why we have these problems in the first place. It's terrible statesmanship to promise voters goodies paid for by future generations, but alas, it's good politics. There's only one way to break the cycle: End the entitlement state.

Social Security was supposed to be an insurance plan for retirement, disability, and survivor benefits. In reality, it was always a Ponzi scheme. It depended on roping ever-more people into the program to cover disbursements. Demographic trends ruined that model. Fortunately, we're not losing much. Social Security's return on investment is about 2 percent higher than inflation. Equities markets over the long run deliver 5-7 percent above inflation. Uncle Sam isn't doing you any favors when it docks your paycheck in exchange for much lower yields than you could've achieved on your own.

Today's financial markets offer many options for brokerage accounts and securities purchases. The proliferation of exchange-traded funds over the past two decades makes diversification accessible even for households of modest means. Government isn't performing an important public service by forcing citizens into an inefficient pension plan. It's continuing a failed program due to political inertia. Let's stop.

Medicare is trickier, since healthcare markets in the U.S. are such a mess. However, that mess is of Uncle Sam's making. Medicare alone accounts for about 20 percent of national health expenditures. At the same time, there are legions of rules on the books that restrict competition. Boosting demand while hindering supply makes things more expensive. Winding down Medicare would ease pricing pressures, but this should be coupled with widespread healthcare deregulation for maximum effect.

An intermediate option—hardly libertarian but at least consistent with American federalism—is to devolve health care policy to the states. Put the responsibility for qualification, payments, and financing in the hands of governors and state legislators, who citizens can more easily control than national politicians and bureaucrats. This would also encourage experimentation. The states have been called "laboratories of democracy" because we can see what works through trial and error. Given the high stakes of healthcare policy, we desperately need competition and innovation. Some states might retain an expansive role for government, like the 2006 Massachusetts plan that inspired Obamacare. Others might privatize the system. Policy diversity is a good thing! We get little useful feedback from one big experiment, but lots from 50 smaller ones.

These proposals may seem radical, but desperate times call for desperate measures. Ignoring the approaching entitlement cliff is totally irresponsible. Business as usual isn't an option. We're running out of time to fix some of the biggest policy errors in American history. If we fail, we're in for a world of economic and political hurt. But if we succeed, we will restore the character of a free society and make the public richer and healthier, besides.

YEARNING TO BREATHE FREE:
Immigration and Liberty

Many Californians are moving to Texas, which has native Texans worried. The Texas model of limited government, fiscal responsibility, and a light regulatory touch has produced great economic prosperity. California, in contrast, is stagnating. Activist government and incomprehensible regulations are driving labor and capital out of the state. Won't all these Californians coming to Texas bring their preferences for nanny-statism with them? Perhaps we should think twice before we let in migrants with very different beliefs and cultures from our own... and think three times before we let them vote.

It sounds compelling. There's just one problem: Our mental model of emigrant Californians is all wrong. We have pretty good data on the political preferences of Californians seeking greener pastures in Texas, as well as similar states like Florida and Iowa. As it turns out, California's "economic migrants" are much more supportive of limited government and free markets than native Texans! Just look at their voting patterns in recent elections. The whole reason they're leaving is because they want more freedom, not less. If liberty-loving Texans are wise, they will welcome West Coast expatriates with open arms.

What's true about migration within the country is true about migration into the country. For all its faults, the United States is a bastion of freedom and tolerance. Millions of people from places like Cuba and Venezuela want to come here and would if they could. In contrast, very few Americans want to put down roots in Caracas or Havana. The reason is obvious: Liberty works, tyranny doesn't. Immigration is a filter that selects for those chasing the American dream.

Immigration reform should be a priority for those who believe in freedom. Mankind's natural rights to "life, liberty, and the pursuit of happiness" imply the right to earn a living with willing employers and raise a family with willing neighbors. It's wrong to use the coercive power of government to prevent those seeking a better life from finding it here.

America has always been a beacon for the rest of the world. Our way of life attracts those yearning for freedom. Those who risk the difficult (and often life-threatening) journey to get here aren't looking to go on the dole. They're looking for independence, responsibility, and industry. We should help them.

Many American citizens, especially Texans, are watching the crisis at our border with alarm. U.S. Customs and Border Protection is overwhelmed. They've encountered more than 2 million immigrants crossing the border in 2022 alone. It's reasonable to wonder whether we have the capacity for much larger immigration levels. Despite appearances, we do. The disaster of our immigration system is a policy choice. We can and must fix it.

Current policy combines the worst of both worlds: Tight restrictions with erratic enforcement. This explains why so many criminal enterprises (traffickers, drug dealers, etc.) are thriving. Since coming here legally is difficult, those desperate for a better life in America must rely on those with specialized skills in evading and resisting law enforcement to get them across the border. The results, mass lawlessness and overwhelmed border communities, are as predictable as they are tragic.

Sensible reforms would make it much easier to live and work here. CBP needs more resources for monitoring, processing, and enforcement. Local communities, from Rio Grande City to El Paso, need upgraded infrastructure to provide basic services. But these must be done with a view to increasing immigration, not restricting it. The only way to make migrant-friendly policies politically viable is to promote a system capable of handling much larger volumes of immigration in a safe and orderly manner.

I can already hear the objections. *Immigrants commit more crime!* No, they don't. Immigrant crime is much less frequent than native crime. *Immigrants take native jobs and lower native wages!* No, they don't. Immigrant labor and native labor are largely complements, not substitutes. *Immigrants abuse the welfare system!* No, they don't. The costs of providing federal entitlements to immigrants is substantially lower than natives. It's reasonable to work for a better system to distribute the costs and benefits of immigration more equitably. But it's not reasonable to exaggerate the costs and diminish the benefits, using these as an excuse for inaction.

We have nothing to fear from immigration and everything to gain. Immigrants strengthen our nation economically and politically. Welcoming them is an obvious boon for liberty. Offering freedom-seekers across the world a safe haven is one of America's oldest and best traditions. Let's all remember the words inscribed at the base of the Statue of Liberty:

Give me your tired, your poor,
Your huddled masses yearning to breathe free,
The wretched refuse of your teeming shore.
Send these, the homeless, tempest-tost to me,
I lift my lamp beside the golden door!

AMERICAN EMPIRE IS THE DEATH OF LIBERTY

Liberty or empire? The foreign policy we choose reflects the kind of nation we want to be. Either we model our values for the rest of the world, or we try to impose them by force. There is no middle ground. Any point on the seesaw between self-governance and imperialism will inevitably tilt towards the latter. If Americans want to keep their freedom, they should heed the advice of George Washington: "steer clear of permanent alliances with any portion of the world" and pursue "harmony [and] liberal intercourse with all nations."[28] It's not our job to boss other countries around or serve as their patrons.

Washington wasn't a small-government fanatic. In fact, he was among the leading advocates of a stronger, more centralized government. But when it came to war and peace, he knew his stuff. Sadly, America didn't take our first president's advice. We now have 750 military bases in 80 countries. We spend more on the military than China, India, the United Kingdom, Russia, France, Germany, Saudi Arabia, Japan, and South Korea *combined.* Our stance towards the international community oscillates between Arlington's brazen hectoring and Foggy Bottom's sanctimonious preaching. This isn't how a responsible nation behaves.

---

28 George Washington. 1796. "The Address of Gen. Washington to the people on His Declining the Presidency of the United States." *Claypoole's American Daily Advertiser,* September 19.

Hubris drives imperialism. American policymakers arrogantly believe they have the power to mold other countries in their image. Our 20-year fiasco in Afghanistan shows this is folly. As we learned from $2.3 trillion in wasted spending and hundreds of thousands of lives lost, nation-building doesn't work. Ideological crusades have left us poorer, weaker, and less free.

Some imperial apologists claim the *Pax Americana* stems from Divine Providence. They should read Holy Scripture more carefully. Israel's history is a record of ruinous encounters with empires: Slavery in Egypt; captivity in Assyria and Babylon; subjugation under Greece and Rome. God uses empires for His own purposes, but that does not make them virtuous. We should not emulate these testaments to man's greed and ambition. Instead, we should embrace the vision of the Prophet Micah: "Nation shall not lift up a sword against nation, neither shall they learn war any more. But they shall sit every man under his vine and under his fig tree; and none shall make them afraid: For the mouth of the LORD of hosts hath spoken it."

There is genuine evil in the world. That much is obvious. But it is not America's responsibility to wield the sword of justice on behalf of mankind. To paraphrase John Quincy Adams, our sixth president, we ought not venture "abroad, in search of monsters to destroy." The quest will eventually corrupt us. Many well-intentioned people want America to protect the world. They don't realize this means they want America to *dominate* the world. For lovers of liberty, this is unacceptable. We cannot abide the hypocrisy of respecting man's rights at home while trampling them abroad.

But aren't foreign interventions necessary to protect domestic freedom? Hardly. In fact, interventionism stifles freedom. As Professors Christopher Coyne and Abigail Hall argue in their recent book, *Tyranny Comes Home*, militarism allows Uncle Sam to experiment with forms of social control in other countries that would be impermissible here.[29] Eventually they "import" these

29 Christopher J. Coyne and Abigail R. Hall. 2018. *Tyranny Comes Home: The Domestic Fate of U.S. Militarism.* Stanford University Press.

techniques to our shores, resulting in privacy-destroying surveil-
lance and an imperious police state. This "boomerang effect" means
violations of foreigners' rights leads to violations of citizens' rights.

The United States is supposed to be a democratic republic.
But as with democratic Athens and republican Rome, our elites
intend to sacrifice the body politic on the altar of imperialism. If
we want to remain free, we must completely change our foreign
policy. The default should be political neutrality and economic
liberalism. Goods, persons, and ideas should cross our borders
with ease. Our military should be strong enough to deter invasion
and protect shipping, and no stronger. Alliances with nations of
goodwill to protect our mutual interests are appropriate, so long
as they are specific and conditional. Above all, our dealings with
other countries should be honest and humble.

We are not the world's conscience, still less its policeman.
President Adams said it best: America "is the well-wisher to the
freedom and independence of all," but "the champion and vindicator
only of her own."[30]

---

30 John Quincy Adams. 1821. "An address, delivered at the request of the committee of
arrangements for celebrating the anniversary of Independence, at the City of Washington
on the Fourth of July 1821 upon the occasion of reading The Declaration of Independence."
July 4.

TO THE STARS! LIBERTY ON THE FINAL FRONTIER

The prospects for liberty here on Planet Three look grim. Global authoritarianism is on the rise. Even in liberal-democratic countries, the scale and scope of government permanently expands. Instead of solutions to vital social problems, we get sinecures for the managerial-administrative class. Liberty is getting squeezed everywhere we look. There's a chance citizens can use political processes to reverse this. But the odds are long.

Perhaps we should form new political institutions instead of reforming old ones. But where? The planet's real estate is almost entirely monopolized by governments. They won't be eager to accommodate pro-liberty communities within their domain. Even if they did initially, there's nothing stopping them from reneging on the deal afterwards. We're living in the future President Reagan warned us about: "If we lose freedom here, there's no place to escape to. This is the last stand on earth."

So let's not look on earth. A solution both simple and fantastic presents itself: Outer space can be the new home for lovers of liberty. Thomas Paine, America's greatest polemicist, famously wrote, "We have it in our power to begin the world over again." The greater our capacity to venture into space, the closer that power becomes.

Space is an ideal setting for new communities dedicated to freedom. Public international space law prevents nation-states from extending their territorial jurisdiction to the moon, Mars, and other celestial bodies. The foundational legal document is the 1967 Outer Space Treaty, signed by all the major spacefaring nations.[31] Article II of this treaty reads, "Outer space, including the moon and other celestial bodies, is not subject to national appropriation by claim of sovereignty, by means of use or occupation, or by any other means." This quasi-anarchic domain provides the perfect opportunity for social and political entrepreneurs to experiment with new ways of living.

The first space communities will likely focus on extracting and refining resources. Asteroids contain rare mineral deposits that boggle the mind in terms of market value.[32] Water can be used to make new rocket fuel, which no longer needs to be hauled beyond earth's gravity well.[33] Surely we'll need a system for defining and enforcing property rights. Since governments can't do it, space communities themselves will, likely through voluntary, bottom-up processes for adjudicating disputes—a new system of private commercial law in space.[34] Just as the common law was once a bulwark against rapacious governments on earth, private law can protect life, liberty, and property in our ventures to the stars.

Celestial property rights are an important step towards a permanent legal order.[35] Unlike previous experiments in ordered liberty, foremost among them the American Founding, there will probably not be a "constitutional moment" marking the conscious acceptance of a "social contract" for space.[36] Instead, the rules will emerge gradually, as parties seek timely, cost-minimizing ways to resolve disputes. While the principles of liberty are universal, institutions for defending liberty work best when they arise in discrete steps, subject to trial-and-error along the way.

31 United Nations. 1966. "Treaty on Principles Governing the Activities of States in the Exploration and Use of Outer Space, including the Moon and Other Celestial Bodies." December 19.

32 Martin Armstrong. 2022. "The Colossal Untapped Value of Asteroids." Statistica, June 30.

33 Ella Anderson. 2020. "Making Rocket Fuel from Water." *Predict*, December 19.

34 Alexander William Salter. 2020. "Outer space needs private law." *The Space Review*, August 31.

35 Alexander William Salter. 2020. "Celestial property rights." *SpaceNews*, August 3.

36 Michael S. Greve. 2012. "Constitutional Moments." *Law & Liberty*, October 1; Celeste Friend. 2004. "Social Contract Theory." Internet Encyclopedia of Philosophy, October 15.

Freedom means running many simultaneous experiments to discover the best ways to live. As the body of rules determining resource use and exchange grows, the ways we can combine those resources to form durable communities will multiply. Similar processes often began on earth, but always invited predation by governments and their monopolistic proclivities. But in space, as we've seen, states' ability to suppress these experiments is highly limited. If a terrestrial nation attempts to quash celestial communities, other nations will immediately raise objections. No spacefaring nation wants to see its rivals extend their coercive domain. For once, the game of international power struggles can work in liberty's favor.

Elon Musk, the mercurial CEO of SpaceX, was fiercely criticized for declaring Mars "a free planet" and denying any "Earth-based government has authority or sovereignty over Martian activities."[37] But this is a straightforward description of public international space law, not a manifesto for techno-corporate tyranny. Nation-states will continue their descent into bureausclerosis. Thankfully, the space agreements they forged in decades past laid the groundwork for a new era of freedom. Private entities, whether profit-seeking or not, will play a pivotal role in founding space communities. The way of the future is a constellation of private-governance providers.

Frontiers have always beckoned freedom-seekers. The final frontier will eclipse them all.

---

37 Alexander William Salter. 2020. "Elon Musk's Martian Way (Empire not Included)." *National Review*, November 12.

23

AMERICAN LIBERTY IN THE 21ST CENTURY

For a year and a half, I had the pleasure of defending America's philosophy of liberty in the *Lubbock Avalanche-Journal*. My first column in this series, "Conserving liberty: Why libertarianism deserves a hearing," appeared on July 4, 2021. It was quite a journey! Thanks to my editors, Doug Hensley and Adam Young, for encouraging me to write these articles. And of course, thanks to my readers. Your attention, consideration, and engagement made it all worthwhile.

Conclusions are a good place to sum up. In that spirit, I'd like to leave you with a reminder of what we've learned:

American conservatives must conserve the Founding. What should conservatives conserve? The answer depends on their heritage and traditions. For Americans, the object of conservation is the Founding. Although it seems paradoxical, American conservatives must be liberals at heart, because the American Revolution was a liberal revolution dedicated to securing man's natural rights of life, liberty, property, and the pursuit of happiness. Remember: "Liberal" does not mean "left-wing." The root of the word "liberal" means "freedom." Liberty is at the heart of what it means to be an American.

Liberty, not license. All true liberty is ordered liberty. Freedom ultimately means the right to do one's duty. As human beings, we recognize our obligations to God, our families, our local communities, and our nation. Government promotes human flourishing by limiting itself to protecting our natural rights. Other communal organizations—churches, universities, fraternal societies—exist to fulfil man's social nature and help him become virtuous. The government's role is securing freedom.

Government is inherently violent. We previously discussed the phrase, "Government is just another name for the things we do together." This sounds nice, but it's baloney. We engage in non-governmental collective action all the time. If you're a member of a country club, a church council, or a nonprofit committee, you've participated in "the things we do together." What distinguishes government is not collectivity, but coercion. Government is violence, plain and simple. Only the government may initiate violence against otherwise peaceful persons. To protect our natural rights, this power must be held in check. Written constitutions, the rule of law, and democracy are all ways to limit the government to its proper protective function.

Libertarianism can end our political arms race. America's government has gotten too big and tries to do too much. This causes partisan polarization. When the stakes of politics get too high, our neighbors' political preferences may become a threat to our preferred way of life. This turns friends into enemies. To lower the stakes, we need to embrace a philosophy of liberty. Libertarianism can solve our polarization problem by strictly limiting the acceptable scope of politics. Many social problems should be solved through *voluntary* collective action. We should turn to the government only if there's no other choice.

Liberty is social; coercion is anti-social. King Stephen I of Hungary, venerated as a saint in both the Christian East and West, wisely counseled his people, "A nation of one language and the same customs is weak and fragile." In other words, a nation is a community of communities. Each of those communities is devoted to a moral good, and perhaps even the highest good, God. It is inevitable that these communities will disagree, as we've always disagreed about the nature of a life well-lived.

Yet even communities with very different moral commitments can live together in harmony if they respect the dignity of human persons. The government's job is to serve as a referee, ensuring no community violates our God-given natural rights. Libertarianism is a profoundly social philosophy because it guards the foundations of authentic community.

The future is freedom. America confronts enormous challenges. The economy is stagnant. The dollar rapidly depreciates. Federal spending, especially entitlement programs, bankrupts the nation. Hostile powers abroad threaten our peace and security, the Chinese Communist Party chief among them. Despite these problems, America can flourish if we rediscover the value of liberty. Slashing regulations and curbing the Federal Reserve can restore our economy. Spending restraint and entitlement restructuring can put us on a fiscally sustainable path. We can't beat China by adopting their heavy-handed form of authoritarian capitalism, but we can by embracing America's traditional free-market dynamism. Undoubtedly, we need capable public servants to spearhead these reforms. But We the People must move them to action. A 21st century policy agenda must embrace America's governing philosophy, not retreat from it. We want America to flourish *as America*—the world's greatest experiment in ordered liberty.

Are we still worthy of the Founders' patrimony? I believe so. The renaissance of American liberty can start right now, provided we hold fast to what makes our country unique. Only by putting freedom first can we achieve greatness and equality. Join me in preserving what sets America apart from the mass of ordinary nations.

CONCLUSION

If this book gave its readers a greater appreciation for the relevance of libertarianism to American politics, it achieved its purpose. But this is not the last word on liberty and public affairs. In fact, there is no such thing. Self-governance means an ongoing conversation about how we order our lives together. The ideas in this book should help readers participate in that conversation.

In that spirit, I'd like to offer some concluding thoughts about liberty. They are suggestions for putting libertarianism to work. Having come this far, readers undoubtedly have their own thoughts about freedom, virtue, and politics. They may differ markedly from my own. If the disagreements result in fruitful tensions and productive exchanges, so much the better.

Our basic conception of liberty can be "immanent" or "transcendental." The former views society as essential for securing the blessings of liberty, which is best pursued gradually within existing institutions. The latter views society as potentially stifling liberty, which is a moral claim against existing institutions. Americans are the proud inheritors of a revolutionary tradition. We cannot totally disavow transcendental liberty. Nevertheless, my own views (discernible, I hope, in many of the chapters) favor immanent liberty. Make no mistake: Natural rights exist, always and everywhere. But the ways we defend them depends heavily on culture, prudence, and statesmanship. Furthermore, revolutions have a lousy track record. 18th century America is an outlier. Much more often, things go the way of 18th century France or 20th century Russia. Precisely because our desired reforms are radical, libertarians' sympathy should lie with those who build up, rather than those who tear down.

Libertarians should not be afraid of "doing" politics. Oftentimes, libertarians view involvement in public affairs with suspicion. Engaging in politics, let alone being good at politics, seems to contradict libertarian values. This is counterproductive. If we want liberty-friendly policy, we need liberty-friendly political operatives. There is a danger here, of course. Passionate advocates of freedom can unwittingly become part of the system they swore to dismantle. But we shouldn't equate deal-making and compromise with betrayal. Unless your strategy is inciting a second American Revolution (bad idea; see above) or convincing a supermajority of citizens to take "What Would Rothbard Do?" buttons with them to the ballot box, you're going to need libertarians who are both principled and pragmatic doing the long, hard, unglamorous work of unwinding Leviathan.

This brings us to something I hardly discussed in the book: Political parties. I'm not interested in telling you what party to support. But I do think there are things a party should do to earn your loyalty. First, an effective political party organizes coalitions to win elections. Education, outreach, and similar functions are important, but they're not what parties are for. If these other goals aren't subordinated to winning elections, the time and effort is misused. Second, an effective political party tries to expand its coalition by persuading people on the margin. The social-media outrage machine makes it easy to forget this point, but we'd better remember if we want to win. A disciplined party won't develop platforms and messaging strategies that "fire up" existing supporters at the cost of alienating potential supporters. Think twice before supporting anybody who doesn't understand the difference between a retweet and a vote.

I began this volume with a warning. The pursuit of "national greatness" by contemporary progressives and conservatives endangers American liberty. It seems fitting to conclude by paying my respects to Patrick Henry, who recognized this problem centuries ago. During Virginia's Ratifying Convention (June 1788), Henry lamented his colleagues' growing enthusiasm for the politics of power and a "great, splendid" government. "When the American spirit was in its youth, the language of America was different; liberty, sir, was then the primary object," he reminded the Convention.[38] As students of the American revolution know, Henry understood the importance of passion and purity. But he also understood the importance of persuasion, organization, and coalition-building. Once again, our politics has lost sight of its "primary object." We will need both kinds of talents to put liberty back in its rightful place.

---

38 Patrick Henry. 1788. "Remarkts at the Virginia Ratifying Convention." June 5.

ABOUT ALEXANDER WILLIAM SALTER

Alexander William Salter is the Georgie G. Snyder Associate Professor of Economics in the Rawls College of Business and the Comparative Economics Research Fellow with the Free Market Institute, both at Texas Tech University. He has authored or coauthored three books: *Money and the Rule of Law* (Cambridge University Press), *The Political Economy of Distributism* (Catholic University of America Press), and *The Medieval Constitution of Liberty* (University of Michigan Press). In addition to his numerous scholarly articles, he has published nearly 400 opinion pieces in leading national outlets such as the *Wall Street Journal*, *National Review*, *Fox News Opinion*, and *The Hill*.

Salter earned his M.A. and Ph.D. in Economics at George Mason University and his B.A. in Economics at Occidental College. He was an AIER Summer Fellowship Program participant in 2011.

ABOUT AIER

The American Institute for Economic Research in Great Barrington, Massachusetts, was founded in 1933 as the first independent voice for sound economics in the United States. Today it publishes ongoing research, hosts educational programs, and is home to the Bastiat Society. The American Institute for Economic Research is a 501c3 public charity.

Made in the USA
Middletown, DE
23 July 2023